B

C000021630

ANTONY DUNN was born in Lor
gate Prize in 1995 and received
Award in 2000. He has published two collections of poems, *Pilots and Navigators* (Oxford*Poets* 1998) and *Flying Fish* (Carcanet/Oxford*Poets* 2002). He has worked on a number of translation projects with poets from Holland, Hungary, China and Israel, and was Poet in Residence at the University of York for 2006. He also writes for the theatre and his plays include *Dog Blue*, *Goose Chase* and *Shepherds' Delight*. His website is www.antonydunn.org.

Also by Antony Dunn from Carcanet Press/OxfordPoets

Pilots and Navigators
Flying Fish

ANTONY DUNN

Bugs

Oxford*Poets*

CARCANET

Acknowledgements

Beads on the Tongue (ed. Silvestar Vrljić, Brutal/Kigen, Zagreb 2008), *Dreamcatcher*, *English Review*, *Grimsby Evening Telegraph*, *In the Criminal's Cabinet* (ed. Val Stevenson and Todd Swift, nthposition 2004), *The Journal*, *The Manhattan Review*, *Nightingale*, *Oxford Poetry*, *Oxford Today*, *PN Review*, *Poetry and Audience*, *Poetry London*, *Poetry Review*, *Quadrant* (Australia), *Radio Waves* (ed. Seán Street, Enitharmon 2004), *The Slab*, *Stand*, *The Third Way*, www.nthposition.com, www.thepoem.co.uk. 'Girl with Gun, Ben Gurion Airport' was broadcast on BBC Radio 3's *The Verb* in June 2007.

'Antimony Cup' was commissioned by the Poetry Book Society on behalf of the Victoria and Albert Museum, London, and is here dedicated to the memory of Michael Donaghy. 'Platform Announcements' was commissioned by Nicola Breslin to accompany an exhibition of her photographs of Norwich railway station. 'Eyeglass' and 'Us All' were inspired by Bridget Foreman's script for Riding Lights Theatre Company's *Science Friction*. 'Bread Line' was written for Riding Lights' play *Hope Opera*.

Thanks to the Arts Council of England, the Arvon Foundation, the British Council, Cove Park, the Pushkin Trust; to Julia Bird, Andrew Collier, Susan Elderkin, Jane and David Searle, Hilary and Oliver Simon; to Polly Clark, Julia Copus, Clare Pollard and Owen Sheers; to Matthew Hollis and Vicki Hackett for the above and beyond.

First published in Great Britain in 2009 by
Carcanet Press Limited
Alliance House
Cross Street
Manchester M2 7AQ

A CIP catalogue record for this book is available from the British Library
ISBN 978 1 903039 95 3

The publisher acknowledges financial assistance from Arts Council England

Typeset by XL Publishing Services, Tiverton
Printed and bound in England by SRP Ltd, Exeter

Contents

Thou shalt not nede to be afrayed for eny bugges by night.

Psalm 91:5, Coverdale's Bible, 1535

If all the matter in the universe except the nematodes were swept away, our world would still be dimly recognizable… we should find its mountains, hills, vales, rivers, lakes, and oceans represented by a film of nematodes… Trees would still stand in ghostly rows representing our streets and highways. The location of the various plants and animals would still be decipherable, and, had we sufficient knowledge, in many cases even their species could be determined by an examination of their erstwhile nematode parasites.

Nathan A. Cobb, *Yearbook of the United States Department of Agriculture*, 1914

Bugged

The usual suspects, of course – the phone
and the barrel-end of his fountain pen,

the picture frames, reading lamps, ceiling rose –
he's been through them all leaving microphones.

But more; the whole house is listening out.
One stitched in a pillow, one sunk in soap,

spiked in a wine-bottle, tapped in a plug.
And now he himself can't for certain recall

which of the cobwebs on the top-shelf books
is the homespun nanotechnology

which will trap then transmit his every breath.
He's proud of this work he's done in his home

and it's finished, apart from this one last thing:
to wait for what comes in the small-hours' dark;

for the tell-tale scuttling outside the door,
for whoever it is that's been listening in.

He opens his mouth.
                    If you're there, I'll begin.

Flea Circus

When the time came we packed up the Big Top,
stowed it in the trunk and drove off the map.

Back in the dark the glass tent came alive:
trapeze and cannon, plunge-pool and high-wire,

everything shaken to a frenzied show.
And though we'd later accuse – come to blows –

we'd never be sure which of our number
left the Top unhooked; by trick or blunder

let our stars seize the chance, make a clean jump
out through the countless non-doors of the trunk.

But fled they were, for sure, when we arrived.
And though we made the best of it, and thrived,

found ourselves skilled in micro-mechanics,
some of us resented living off tricks

and felt in the itch of our bad-feeling
the bite of our great hope's flight, the bleeding,

the drop-by-drop drain of a life gone thin.
The fleas, somehow, still, get under our skin.

Kitchen Sink Drama

On the one hand, this
is Mark, washing up.

But see here, beyond the pane
above the altar-ware of taps,

that spider again, slubbing
its train of leadwork around the frame,

maker and mender, restless heart
of its own rose window;

libations of rain, spiced
with sulphides and soot,

the transubstantiation of frost
and sun, puzzling out shards of colour;

this work holding house and home
together. So, on the other hand,

this is Mark, offering
his forgetful hands –

a pair of doves –
in a cage of water and knives.

Antimony Cup

It is a poisoned chalice
                    that we raise –
but as we toast each other's healths,
                            and chink
our fragile cups together,
                     let us praise
the nation we're creating
                       with this drink,
as we beget a finer race
                  of men
and draft its customs with this
                     alchemy –
eternal Friday nights
                of swirl and churn
of wine and air in this
               antimony.
We sink a cup to purge what makes us
                          sick,
and sketch out shapes of Empire
                        on the floor
in splash on spreading splash of pink
                       on brick
and blanket; wine and bile. Landlord,
                     one more!
One final shot to get
               under our skin.
Sorry, gents, it's time.
               Better out than in.

Why Did the Chicken

No, we must not joke about these things now:
the Chinese girl in a field who was first
to go when the cocktail went off
in her arms,
            the birdwatchers drafted
to government hides to spy out the swans
and the geese crafting in from the sea
in neutral colours,
            and Radio 4
putting out an appeal to the curtain-
twitchers of Oxfordshire and Gloucestershire
and farther and farther to snitch on the birds
in their own back yards,
               the ravens, hooded
and rushed from the Tower in a blacked-out car
to an underground bunker,
              the kids
of the Ornithologist Youth flushing
every last nut-hatch and tree-creeper out
from the woodwork, into a trackable
tag,
      the embassies under every flag
rolling out the razorwire to stop
the starling, a dirty bomb who'd burst
suddenly out of the mob and in
through a window
           or the Yorkshire trader
who flogs off pigeons he's already trained
to home to *his* home and fold themselves,
at night, back into his loft with a sound
like the riffle of tenners
            but sleeps
through one of them clearing its throat with a cough
that migrates, mutates, a Chinese whisper
among the birds which, tomorrow, will be loosed
in the market place, then zero home to roost.

We apologise for the delay

but two miles up the line
a freight train has broken down

and is weeping diesel
into the shushing snow.

We could whisper past, but
one spark against the rails

could catch, easy as a cold,
and set the slush aflame,

and us. Enjoy the view
and, while the power holds out,

the free melt-water tea
we will be pushing round.

And just before the rising snow
and falling night close down

your widescreen windows, peer
through the crushing weather:

observe the husky team
sledding from the guard's van,

stoking its steam-engine breath,
nosing north and swooshing off.

And, seal-skinned, polar-furred,
me; bossing one new track

into ice and spindrift,
the percussion of dogs

and the lantern's blush trailing
after the rig, then pinched out.

Ladies and gentlemen,
picture me rushing the team

through the aurora, tomorrow's
one poor hour of sunlight,

through Finger Lake, Rainy Pass,
the Kushokwim River;

everything whiting out
through Ophir, Iditarod,

Koyuk, beyond... I may be
some time. Mushing on. So long.

Us All

What's this?

Two naked idiots
in a field,

all bangled with aphids,
snail-tattooed,

skimming the milky grass
for crickets,

scooping up grasshoppers
from tall leaves,

holding them in shelled hands
to their ears

to catch the whispering
of planets,

stars, rattling like pebbles
in small waves

or the spiracle-sigh
of black holes

sucking everything clean
in their pull.

Damping the tuning-forks
of legs, wings,

with a pinch – this they have
discovered.

But splitting cicadas
on thumb-nails

to spill the chirp-works
of their song

and finding nothing there
to explain

the noise, and how it keeps
unspooling,

they're naked idiots
in a heap

of creatures cracked open
in a field,

meaning no harm at all
in the world.

Please

Do not drop coins into the water and wish:
it may pollute the pool and cause infection in the fish.

Berlin Zoo

The polar bear is psychotic, banging
its head bald behind its left ear, as if
there were voices there, all speaking in tongues;
its *umlaut* eyes print-black, unreadable
above the aspirate vowel of its mouth
to the English boy who is here alone.

The neon displays of *Nachtlokalen*
are soaking their coils in the city sun
and he envies the creatures, in this heat,
their buckets of apple-flesh and water.
He would buy a drink from the *Verkäufer*
but can't, the asking balled up in his throat

with the taste of cages – hotel rooms, car,
the bedclothes, the keeper's stink in the dark –
and one thought wears itself threadbare, banging
around his skull, which is how he might spell
the sob in the catch of a lion's cough
or make sense of the howl of gibbon, wolf.

Lisdoonvarna

1942

He'd hook cycle-clips, lucky as horseshoes,
in a black love-heart in his breast pocket
and, having no bicycle nor even
the front to dab his tie with petrol, walk.

September, and the fields lying in wait
for the fire through the stubble and the smoke;
the first drub and craic of drums rolling in
from far off, the pulse of the place racing.

He'll not be dancing, though. He's two left feet
and the unbalance in his chest, the weight
of the ghost of a whale lumped in one lung.
Ten years he's been a fish out of water

since his night waist-deep by the dead creature,
his three days and nights sunk in a fever.
Jonah, they call him, the girls who sniff out
a lift home in the closing of a clinch

or read in the boys' braille of cycle-clips
the promise of a cross-bar through the dark.
Spat up on the shore of the lamplight's wash,
he watches the splash and spume of the dance,

an hour or so, then out to the sea-path,
leaving the whispers of deals done drowned out
by a tide the colour of submarines,
and, pocket wishboned, wishes himself out,

all at sea in a whale's gut; then landfall,
a demon, swine-bound, cast back on dry land.

Ladybird

He was the boy who rolled a ladybird
like a blood-bead around his fingers, wrist,

slowed through the streets to your house with this gift,
kept its path level from elbow to palm.

And he was the boy took a flight of stone
to the forehead for *walking like a spaz*

through the bike-boys, doing that with his arm,
but didn't spill a drop or turn for home.

First Kiss

That's it. In the garage, in your school skirt,
leaning against the Mazda's rust-blue tail,
you were all green eyes, yellow hair cut short
and you were holding the wormery bowl.

Homework of worms going on behind glass:
the clean-cut strata of soil, sand and peat
were blurring already, churned up and cast
through the guts of worms and their appetite.

Yes, I held the wormery bowl, for sure,
while you cooled your thighs on the green Fiat,
eyes blue yes blue, closed under ditch-mud hair.
On the drive. A rust-blue dress. That was it.

Maria

A little water clears her of this deed.

Her skinny wrists cuffed in her mother's grip,
she is salt-scrubbed in surf until the gilts
of scales are loosened from her fingers
with the offal of the stolen fish, pinched
one by one from her brother's line, alive,
and broken in her inquisitive hands.

Cutlery adrift, we are witnesses.
Underneath our table a cat marvels
at the clockwork of a cockroach,
winding it in its teeth, setting it off.
In its green wheelbarrow a sheep, meekly,
considers its bindings and its progress.

★

Maria is fishing, until the sea
hangs on her wire a shock of octopus.
Black-faced in its fearful rage, alien,
it wears her hugely in its bangling arms;
and the sea-creature and earth-creature trap
and trade their horror as if in mirrors

till her brother unclasps the octopus
and turns it inside-out over his thumb;
and her mother tends her in the water,
scrubbing her into chill shackles that slip,
easy, onto her wrists where sweetening air
and clean water fasten. This fastening,

this ink; a tattoo on water, under skin.

Ants

Hay fever season,
        the labourers move,
removal men, a
            pantechnicon-train
hoisting ounces of
        cumin, lemongrass,
peppercorns and rice.

        What are we to do
but boil the kettle
            over and over
and loiter around
        their several ways in
and out, to soften
        their labours like this?

Must be thirsty work
    in that black. Shift work.
They're unquenchable,
        dismantling slack fruit;
cleaning up the pulp,
        the husk and the seed
of this mess we're in.

        Our eyes hot and fierce
with our gratitude,
        we will blink to find
all that makes us weep
        and snivel swept off,
out and underground,
            under our noses.

New Year Instant Poem

In a sky fizzing with fireworks and snow
seagulls turn on time-lags
between the arrivals of light and sound
and the wind takes the colour-bursts apart
like dandelion clocks.

Champagne giddies up the blood. We unstick
a first step out of this
cooling bridge-light, this fixture of amber.
The cork we burst over the river mouth
is hurried off to sea.

Skinny Dipping

We peeled ourselves out of our other skins
and lost our underwear under water,
nymphed about between speedboats and lake-bed.

And later, cast off in our only skins,
we've ploughed through bedbugs heavy as water
and buddy-breathed through these fathoms of bed.

And you mouth and gog at my stomach-skin's
anchored-in tick, then hang in treadwater
to tweeze the first bloodsucker from our bed.

Limequat

A man weeps in a garden centre's nursery
at the weight in his embrace of a citrus tree:

a present to be glared at from the bed, and dared
to *do* something, like Venus Fly Trap, talking bird;

to fatten in the window-heat, the landing light,
to fruit between the thumbs and fingers of his wife

who's home and boiling marmalade or washing jars,
sounding out the space in the empty swells of glass.

He is surprised at this weeping over his gift,
how he dissolves among the tanks of formless fish,

at how he finds so much depends upon it; how
it's going to muscle in, haul its height through greenfly

to outgrow its graft-bandage, make of its hard knots
fruits neither lime nor kumquat, neither this nor that.

But rain is ruffling the evening roof-glass; it's time
to wrap it in a black bin-bag and take it home.

Lepidopterist

He'd like to unfold her from that lab coat
and see what kind of creature she'd become;

chalk up a finger on a butterfly wing
and lay out his great design on white silk –

a dress for her to wear weightlessness in;
or dust his fingerprints across her skin

in kohl and carmine; or see, as she moves
through the store-room, the cases fly open

and every last butterfly unhook itself
and throw itself into the air, and stay.

He'd like the creature cocooned in his chest
to stop turning over – to burst from his mouth

on unspeakable wings. He'd like to say something
that she'd understand, but can't pin it down.

Flight

He would ease these fingerprints off
    with razor blade or Stanley knife,
        flight them free like bees' wings to hang
        looping, bodiless on the breeze,
    while he alights on you with these
untraceable and unringed hands.

Testing One Two

Not a mic taped under her bra
or a button–camera pinned to her coat,

but the doorbell, her red-faced macaw
dudding the mesh and pop-shield of its dome

and her *Would you mind? Are you sure?*
and *I'll pick it up by midnight*, by rote,

or the ring that brings the mynah
in secretary black into his home

to spook his every move at night,
or cockateels to unsettle his guests;

her relay of stumm parakeets
sticking their sticky beaks in secret things,

and how he's grown to learn to hate
the casual way they squawk beneath their breaths,

Who's a pretty boy? to the mites
listening in the lapels of their wings.

Platform Announcements

00:00

The train now slowing into platform one
is a film of you, trapping in the gate,
and the empty glare in the stock-still frame
is where you've melted from, tattered in light.

00:40

Killing time at the cash machine for this:
its green bedside bleeps, long overspent; these
proofs that the pulse of the place is holding,
this measuring the night in tens and twenties.

01:10

The roof-light's a rose window opening
in the highest height of the smoke-dark stone.
I test your name against the hush of it
for the way it's turned about, thrown back down.

02:50 (waiting room)

Locked, it's a crime-scene tent. There on the floor,
invisibly chalked between guilty seats,
the outline of the bag we both went for
at once; the two tracks of our one route out.

04:00

The train not arriving at platform eight
is one a world from here, plunging you home:
husband, sleep-breathing kids; the second you
can't, for the life of you, remember your name.

Cold

Come on then
scoop these blossoms
from the bed

these white blown-petalled
snot-soaked
tissue-heads

and weave
a dewy wreath
that spells my name

to go with me
to black car
   casket
        flame

Unsaid

There will be time for this later.
Just now, though, let it be enough
to find our way through the backwash
of cuttlefish and brittlestars,
the yards of dogfish spine, stripped white
from tail to eyeless head, the claws,
the legs, the gutted hulls of crabs;
to be undone by all of this;
to roil across this tide of stones
through all the gulls have left undone
among the groynes and landing traps;
to know the shuttered sun will come
again, will come again, that we
still make each other out. Let's say
that what we have to say we'll save.
There will be enough time later.

Saguaro

So when at last we are drunk dry
and stand back from the wrung-out keys

the static sparks at finger-ends
turn pins and needles in our hands.

We scale the stairs and go our ways
and find our necessary space,

bed in beneath the too-hot moon,
saguaro-stiff, at every turn

tear up our sheets with prickling skin
and blinklessly endure alone.

So much depends on this, that we
lie cactus-armed and fiercely dry.

If one of us should spill but one
quick drop the way a rain begins,

fingering one high note to warn
its hot disorder in, how soon

we'll find ourselves in bloom, amazed,
the downpour's four hands at the keys

pinning us in sparking sheets, and
this is how it goes – one grand

unseasonable storm, and days
will come and have to drink us dry.

Nettle Bed

Sure and if I were to step barefoot
into the ditch at Annaghmakerrig
there I might make my bed.

How far away you are and how far
have I come, the way the heron off the lake
is come at double speed

toward the moon from its own reflection
sinking beneath the fish and fields,
nettledown, pillowgrass.

Green

Two greenfinches
are in and out
of the wisteria

where we have sat
all this hard morning
with black coffee

far enough
from the nest
of blackbird throats

and the fierce geese
and their green smears
in the green shade

Love Poetry

As if the bee wouldn't sooner hurl itself into a pub–
    garden pint
than knock itself out on the physics of how its wings
    shouldn't bear it up.

As if the bee doesn't know the better ways to employ a
    tongue that long
than droning on about aerodynamics of pollen streams
    and flight paths.

As if the bee would suffer a ceilidh–caller bawling the
    waggling steps
of its geometrics on paving of honey-light, the dusting
    of touch.

As if these bumbling words would do, butting at the
    walls of an upturned glass
when a lift of the lip would set the improbably beating
    creature off.

Hungarian Blessing

for Clare and Richard

Simply that the women hang
their *Yes*, red-ribboned, in the trees;

that two hours in a ringing train
have carried us through miles of this;

that two days later, sleeping out
in sun, you missed the beetles come;

that these *little cows of god*
herded, graze-red, across your limbs;

that they fluttered from your skin,
streamed at your blood-lines' every fork;

that *Yes*, they clappered off to wing
the moment that you blinked and woke.

Three Dartmoor Ponies

And while we're training the camera to fix
for later whatever the warning is
in their slow dissolving breaths, the landmarks
we've spooled behind us – wall, stile, hut-circle,
hollow – jump at the chance to stir themselves
around, and what we find ourselves is lost.

And just before the fear of it soaks through –
trailing our own ungovernable breaths
and up to our knees in whin and water,
the spotless spawn of frogs snapped up by crows –
we wade the deeping hills with vaulting steps.

And the three ponies hang back in the mist
that's thick with the spill of rain, the sound
of a wood hitching up its skirts to move.

Tarn How

for M

Looking back through the blizzard, it is those
two thin pines, broken at the waist and bowed, their brows
against the hardness of the man-made lake,
that stop us. In this snap we hesitate to take
we'll barely make them out. Let's climb on, before spring
unlocks the ice and undoes everything.

Red

for Bill

Oh, we are foolishly stained.
The burst of dye from a sprung
cash case could not have marked us
out so brightly as this juice
from our cherry orchard raid.

Oh, what a moment then,
for the woman in brown silk
to tear past us through Changsheung
toward the green reservoir
wearing her mother rucksacked –

her motorbike so close that
we're done up in two-stroke dust –
and leave us standing, speechless
and absolutely certain
of what it is just passed us by.

Mayfly Sums Up

Just my fucking luck –
born on a summer Sunday
with all the pods shut.

Peace on Earth

Christmas came in mid-October
at half past three in the morning:

a host of impatient angels
from the city council, swooping

tall storeys, window to window
on the golden wings of their hoists

in the unearthly orange light,
fanfaring their great glad tidings –

a chorus of drills and hammers –
notating their song with coloured bulbs.

House by house the sleepy townsfolk
rubbed the unbelief from their eyes,

the streets an advent calendar
of curtains in unlit bedrooms,

and by the time their focus had cleared
the angel-crews had upped and gone

but this remained: the fading song
from the next street down, then the next,

then nothing but the merest hum
from their phosphorescent wake

and one light already on the blink –
the first of the doubtful filaments

to fade and fail and put itself out.

Eyeglass

Galileo turns on the spot,
adoring globes and moons of fruit,
mapping out the constellations
of his garden in the twilight.

He would like to share this moment
with his daughters, *noviciae*,
the twin blacked-out stars whose quick light
goes on arriving from nowhere.

Measuring the mass of the dark
by the gossip of cicadas,
he unlids the eyeglass's eye
and turns its bold gaze on heaven.

He does not bend, nor fit his own
eye to the insatiable lens.
Some say his diabolic art,
or heresy, earned him blindness;

staring into the very face
of creation. Galileo
is satisfied to imagine
Fra Lippo Lippi's brush
                    flicking
about his optic nerve, dabbing
new perspectives of galaxies
on the mind's eye as, they're saying,
he did to his eyeglass lens;

for he knows God has given him this:
an eye still struck with citrus lights,
all the accidental colours
of the forbidden tree of stars.

Ichneumon Wasp

I cannot persuade myself that a beneficent and omnipotent God would have designedly created the Ichneumonidae with the express intention of their feeding within the living body of caterpillars.

Charles Darwin

How to explain this: the wasp under glass
in its alcohol reliquary,

under its devil's chaplain's red and black
its stun-gun stinger, egg-pouch and blow-pipe;

or the numb gnaw of the grub in his skull
that's growing fat on his paralysed faith;

how he's foot-fooled in the aisles of the ship
as it gives in the pitch of salt water;

and how he must step from this hollow nave
at a day, a time he cannot reckon,

lay out what he knows in bottles and jars
on home-shores made strange by what he brings forth.

Pope Boniface's Address

These wretches, who ne'er lived,
Went on in nakedness, and sorely stung
By wasps and hornets.

                    Dante, *Inferno*, Canto III

Whatever else was due to me, not this.
For ever at my back the rattling wings,
not of angels, but of sulphur-jackets;
infernal wasps with trident-headed stings
whose clamour is the vengeful, wordless roar –
through puncture-wounds – of every cleric hung,
of every monk I hammered to the door
of his own church, alive, by his own tongue.

Worse than this unanswerable din, worse
than being jewelled in welts and cloaked in bees,
is you – your pennies paid to tour my curse,
tripping on and off your sober ferries,
your wing-tongued poet-guides all spewing verse
and jabbing out their dainty allegories.

Endless you. May this amuse you, then, and well,
my hot-foot flight around the endless edge of hell.

Connecticut Bees

This state she's in has come through thaws
of frost and almond blossom; now
the beekeeper pushes through
the months' and quarters' undrunk flowers –
dandelion, apple, goldenrod
and aster – to press her ear
to the ribs of the hives and hears
nothing and, in the end, as new snows
work in from Maine and from Vermont,
she trusts that her subjects will be back
next year, that this is how things go,
and knows that she is right, and is wrong.

June the Fourth

GUIDE

It's a short few steps from the hotel
through the hutong to the cricket-house

Stop staring
               it's just the old guy's home
and though it's all done up like New Year
with homespun strings of wicker baubles
it's a hole and no doubt
                      given wings
he'd airlift himself up out of it
heading west along the flyover
that dots and dashes for miles
                   and stops
mid-air somewhere there's nothing to be
above but dust
              which may or may not
be the place where desert and suburbs
will wreck themselves against each other
when the time comes

                You should reel him off
one of your small notes
                they're only good
for bookmarks back home
                  and drive out there
yourself and peel your green cricket out
from its globe and set it off through straw
and stubble and find out for yourself
what it thinks it's got to sing about

CRICKET

Evening after evening the sun
draped its red folds over the dust-fields
and the sickle moon hung idly up

and the small lights that came out were fires
for melting hoes to cymbals and gongs
to shock the sparrows from crops to traps

and the crickets and the locusts
occupied the emptied air above
the drop and scatter and heap of birds

and the farms rang with the dry whet
of limb on limb and the hunger of
all that wore our bones outside our skin

Translate this –
          Once I wanted to write
only about the bottle
         then I
wanted to write about the bottle
and its shadow
         and now I want to
write only about the shadow –
            and
now do you understand

Now the heat has brought the June-bugs out

Anything we cannot name will go
by that name
                    the caterpillars
                                        say
tracking the road and the cockroaches
scuttering pavements or tattering
their shells against the mausoleum
their great leap forward against the wall
and off and underfoot
                              and the Square
is so alive with them
                              look what you
can crush just by falling to your knees

Bread Line

Sarajevo Symphony cellist Vedran Smajlovic plays Albinoni's Adagio
for victims of the Serb siege of the city, September 1992

I

All along the bakery's crumbling wall,
brick dust and mortar a blessing of flour
on our shoulders, we are a cat-gut queue
stretched thin, waiting for what the wind brings down:

to hold the line through bullets and the scent
of bread, the *Sold Out* rumours, the blood's thump
hollow as the tap of a fingernail
on an upturned loaf that says *it is done*.

And now this jester in a concert suit,
in his chair at the head of the bread line.
His cello, his bow, the bow-tie he wears –
the cross of a target pinned to his throat.

The first day he plays with his eyes tight shut
to keep from seeing the sniper's baton
he knows must fall in a flash, to cut short
his slow-rising solo *adagio*.

Spare us this day our daily dead, it says,
over and over, in stained-glass colours
through bombed-out windows; see how it alters
the waste around the queue to the counter.

Twenty-one days, now, and though every day
he knows that, if some of his crowd don't show,
they won't show again, he stays at the head
of the bread line. We go on forever.

II

These measuring spoons that swing from the fist
like altar-boys' censers, or jailers' keys,

are the thing. The ring of truth. How we must
cup up to the bow of the back, always,

of the fellow one stop along the queue,
to show some backbone in an open street,

say, *This is my body, broken for you*
and hung out to prove where the cross-hairs meet;

to stand in line for the baking of bread –
the breaking – the waiting nakedly here

with the flour-ghost souls of the daily dead,
and rising, oh Christ, in the aisle's cross-fire.

Girl with Gun, Ben Gurion Airport

She pulls you from the check-in queue
and has you unpack everything,
your souvenirs and smalls, and opens up
your laptop, key by key, to make
a scrabble for the X-ray screen.
You're clean.
But all the oleander miles from Tel Aviv,
Ramallah and Jerusalem,
in the back seat of the taxi
you've been swallowing your words
in tiny, tidy packages.
Sit tight.
The taxiing is done.
Ignore the balling of your gut.
This must not split nor spill
a second sooner than its time.

Phantoms

1982

Antonia stealthed a dead locust
under my collar and down my back.
The spine-shiver was like the tremors
from her father, the Phantom pilot,
one of those who'd rattle the locusts
in their sun-bulbed cells around the lab
as he clattered from airfield to air
up rungs of vapour and solid sound.

Summer term: in a wide blue daydream
the tanks blow open and the locusts,
skittering their vertical take-off,
deploy scattered and low. They're smart-bombs
over the gingham green of Sports Day,
the women, children and sandwiches,
cleansing Tupperware and melon-shells,
their hunger scorching the very grass.

Still that itch down the wire of my spine:
the static and white noise of broadcasts
massing; weightless as that locust-corpse
in my palm, in its desert-fatigues
and compound goggles. Or the shadows
that swarmed off the bone-blue slope of sky,
unloading across the fun and games
from Spitfire, Lancaster, Hurricane,

that year as every year, days before
we retreat, go home, grow up, come back.

Taking the Night Air

The kitchen radio
     guides in the air–strike news
through the open window;
     what light creeps out shows
that bats are abroad
     in their black camouflage,
cleansing the air, yard by yard,
     of blips on their radar.

Ultraviolet

Exodus 8:16–19

Our living room windows
were filled with hearth orange
or screen-saver green,
the blue of our wide-screens.

Now they're trapped with blacklight
as the sun drags the night
down upon itself. Gnats
are finding their way in

around blinds and shutters.
The hearths are plagued with ash
and the TVs unplugged:
our insectocutors

blacken and crack with bugs
switched on in the UV
that, in our darkness, we've
dragged down upon ourselves.

They say it's a forecast
of hungrier weather
swarming over the tents,
the settlements lit up

with their payloads of light –
the small, pale suns rising.

Alarm

Blame the apocalypse-cart
that sweeps down Fossgate, early,
to howl us townsfolk out of bed.
We heard it coming streets away –
Stonegate, Petergate, Pavement –
sucking up the last-night mess
we'd scattered round our homes.

Or blame its ear-muffed driver –
who knows? – who never noticed
how he nudged a skew-parked Merc
and set it wailing in his wake,
or how that set its neighbour off,
startled blinking out of sleep
by the first sob of its own alarm.

Either way, the bug was out
and it leapt from car to car
along one orange-sparking street.
And it all blew up from here:
the caterwaul as every house
and every shop tipped off the next
to bawl in dread of fire or theft.

By the time the dawn pulled through
the chorus of alarms was upped
by ambulances, fire engines,
unmanned in their parking bays;
air-raid sirens, cracking rust
from corners of their yawning mouths.
Sparrows were the first brought down.

Pets went quickly round the bend.
The news was lost in closedown bleeps
and testcard whines. We went to ground.
Bunkered in our cellars, fingers
in our ears, we heard the truth creep in:
by road by rail our sound licked out,
sounding out the speed of sound.

But, praying to outlive the lives
of batteries, we couldn't guess
how, up top, lanes of chorus-lines
of ghosted trucks piped up,
this vehicle is reversing,
this vehicle is reversing,
this vehicle is reversing;

or how the sound had reached the coasts
and set the ferries yelping off
to sea; or how the larger mammals
were beginning to succumb;
or how our globe must look from space –
bright as a panic button
in the deafening distance.

Mosquitoes

That was no more than the sound
of night unzipping itself
to admit the wakeful guilts
and terrors. Nothing less.

If you should wake, aloft
on the hard sheet, hands and feet
frayed and fixed in points of blood,
in a storm of bugs,

turn onto your opened side.
Staunch. Unfold the bedclothes. Rise.
There is nothing there, but they
will not be waved away.

Riding Lights

Afterwards, the earth will rig itself
with ropes of fireflies

and drag its anchor from its pitching bed,
heave away at speed

to the ultraviolet horizon of
all that's visible,

signalling in the soundless fizz and flare,
the down-curve and douse

of the crawling constellation of it,
you are here.

Nematode Worms

And after even this, we might
give up a ghost of nematodes;

shrug off a shadow of our streets,
cathedrals, boulevards and zoos,

and set adrift our second skin,
our brittle exoskeleton;

and all that will survive of us
is bugs – these bugs – these parasites;

our lung-light cloud sighed out, as if
the dust of all our equations

of physics and astronomy
were swiped from a blackboard and blown

from one quick bang of a chalk-cloth
hard against a new-swept dark.

Ω

And yet a light is coming in from very far away
My Love, O Love come soon
Even at the last, stop with a kiss this faithless mouth
No, I will not be afraid